Footprints and Verses

Poems of Journey, Adventure and Resilience

Laxmi Singh

BookLeaf
Publishing

India | USA | UK

Made with ❤ on the BookLeaf Publishing Platform
www.bookleafpub.in
www.bookleafpub.com

Dedication

"To all the mothers who journey through chaos and light, may these words be a testament to your strength and love."

Acknowledgement

Thank you to everyone who encouraged me towards my writing journey and for their unwavering love and support. To my friends, whose strength inspired these poems. Special thanks to my friend, Pramod and mentors for their guidance. And to my readers, whose connection to these words makes this journey rewarding.

Preface

As I embarked on this poetic journey, I sought to capture the essence of a mother's adventure, her moments of self-reflection, and the indomitable fighting spirit that defines her path. This collection of poems is a tribute to the resilience, love, and courage that mothers exhibit every day.

Through the ups and downs, the joy and pain, the moments of doubt and the triumphs, these verses reflect the multifaceted nature of motherhood. Each poem is a testament to the strength that lies within, a strength that shines brightly even in the darkest of times.

It is my hope that these words resonate with you, offering inspiration, and a sense of connection. Whether you are a mother yourself, or simply someone who admires the beauty of a mother's journey, may you find pieces of your own story within these pages.

Thank you for joining me on this adventure. May we all continue to navigate life's challenges with grace, hope, and unwavering determination.

Hope!

In the midst of chaos,
Behind the wall of doubts,
You'll stumble upon an element called hope,
And navigate the route, despite the shouts.
Sometimes dark, sometimes darker still,
Blurred milestones and faded dreams,
Subliming fate and suppressed screams,
Yet hold on tight, with iron will.
Sobbing or sulking, there will be moments,
There will be grief, there will be pain,
But through the storm and heavy rain,
Hope remains, a beacon's light,
Guiding you through the endless night.
With resilience strong and spirit unbowed,
A mother's journey through the crowd,
Her heart's whispers, tender and proud,
Emerging victorious, breaking the shroud.

Dear past

One morning, you would see that you are
feeling quite strong,
You accepted the flaws that your fate brought
in and that you were nowhere wrong!

You will be holding the cup of tea, the faded
but resilient blue tea cup by your side,
sipping it slowing with the flashback from the
past on your mind,
But this time, it won't be about the lament,
the grief or the pain from yesterday,
It won't be about the struggle, the losses and
the weaknesses you experienced,
But it will be the about the hope, the passion,
the strength you've gathered so far,
It will be about the selfbelief, the lessons,
looking up high towards the raised bar!

As you gulp the warm tea, you would realize
that your throat nomore chokes,
The thoughts of uncertainty, the taunts of
loved ones are not able to touch your skin,
They come ....but slyly, pass by!

And when you take a deep breath after your
first sip, you notice that it is no more like a
sigh,
Your eyebrows are not perplexed but curious,
your eyes are not wandering but gazing at the
clear sky,
Your face is not pale or weary, it is calm and
relaxed,

That morning you know that your past isn't
your companion anymore,
You have left it behind, it tries really hard to
be a part of your life but fails,

To my past,
Keeping the cup aside, my legs crossed and
my hand on its shoulder,
You have been hovering over me all this while
but Mate,
I know you have been giving it a good try, but
high hopes,
it is finally time to say good bye!

Har Ki Doon: A Mythical Journey

From Sankri's narrow trail, our journey did commence,
Through valleys lush and green, nature's true essence.
The cheerful group, sharing stories from their past,
Developing a bond which will forever last.
Har Ki Doon, the valley of gods, a sacred path we tread,
Following ancient trails, where myth and legend spread.
Along the river's gentle flow, our spirits intertwined,
With tales of Pandavas' journey, their legacy enshrined.
Locals passing by, smiling and giggling,
The simplicity was just so mind boggling,
Through dense forests and meadows vast, a trek of yore,
Echoes of epic battles and stories, forever more.

The river sang its lullaby, a melody pure and
clear,
Guiding us through landscapes, pristine and
austere.
Each step a testament to strength, a tribute to
the past,
In the shadows of the mighty peaks, we
walked steadfast.
Through Osla's charming village, with warmth
and tales so grand,
Where folklore whispered secrets, etched in
the land.
The mighty Swargarohini, its snow-clad peaks
so high,
Watched over us as guardians, beneath the
azure sky,
On our way back, went to the nearby
temples,
The locals were dressed grand, engrossed in
their rituals,
Towards the end, we stood outside, gazing at
the star,
Wondering how beautiful the trails were,
the Swargarohini, now looked pretty far!

Hymn of the mountain

     "I am standing here, been years and
years,
     Wearing my crown higher up,
becoming bigger and bigger,
     a bit scary, but thrilling, snowy and
rocky,
     Keeping my head up, confident and
strong!!! I can see the clouds,
     I can touch the sky, I can see the
world and I can feel the pain,
     I can see your dreams, I can see how
you make them,
     sometimes I see them break!
     It rains and rains and it is cold out
here,
     It is calm at times but clamor at
times,
     I am becoming bigger and bigger,
     but all that matters to me is the
unconditional care,
     I am the shelter for the ones who
respect

) Who values what nature is, who values
what I am
Who values who they are!
It can cost your life; you may never
reach the summit,
You may sit at a rock side and pray till
you die,
You may push yourself harder and
imbibe the holy presence,
You may take an extra step and move
inch by inch
You may sit and quit, you may lose
and feel the pinch
You may look higher and higher, you
need to dedicate and commit
If you embrace life and if you aim the
summit,
You will keep going and keep walking
and walking,
till you see nothing in front but the
summit!"

In the Midst of Chaos

The darkness is existing,
 The chaos is persisting,
 In hope to be able to go home soon,
 I stay back and gaze at the blurred moon!
Children singing and playing,
 Couples holding hands and walking by the
side,
 Shops are crowded, roads are bustling,
 Lanes are full, friends are sitting at cafés,
talking and laughing,
 Loud music spills from a lively and dreamy
pub,
 I rub my tired eyes,
 And wonder—
 Will it ever be the same again?

Let go!

I was not holding anyone.
It wasn't until I opened my arms that I realized: I was holding nothing.
 No burden, no weight, no chains. Only emptiness.
 Grains of sadness had once clung to me, my life tangled in invisible strings, forces pulling me in every direction.
 But when I finally let go, I discovered the ground beneath me was not solid—I was standing on a mountain of sand.

Always look up and seek the light.
It doesn't matter how many times you've failed, as long as you're ready to rise and fight again.
 You may have fallen. You may feel broken.
 But you can always stand tall again.
 Pace doesn't matter. Hope does. And with hope, you can reach any height.
It may seem dark—or even darker still. But remember this: after every long night, there will be a dawn.

I slipped into the tunnel of despair. But in that stillness, all I could do was embrace change. Rise, reflect, but always move forward.

It doesn't matter how weak you feel, as long as you keep fighting, the battle goes on.

I could feel life again. The thrill of hope, the strength of persistence.

It is only when I opened my heart that I realized—

I was not holding anyone.

Reflections at Shanti Stupa

As I sat holding my cup of tea, gazing at the
horizon,
The lavender petals waving as the wind sets in
motion,
Yellow pollen inside, reflecting the color of
the sun,
Guest houses looked so tiny from above, like
dreams undone.
The air getting colder, cheerful children
nearby, Subliming sunrays,
the day's final goodbye, The place looks the
same, as if I was here yesterday!
Shanti Stupa, a serene embrace for tourists in
Leh's sway.
White as clouds, blue and purple designs at
its base,
The mighty Buddha inside, a calm and sacred
space,
A panoramic view that leaves one in a daze!
The garland of mountains, the green patch of
Ganglas.

Winding trails nearby, weaving stories
untold,
Into thin air, yet feels so full, bold and old,
As night falls, the Stupa stands, tranquil and
grand,
Holding moments of peace in its silent hand.

By the Ghats of Banaras

The magenta hues of the mesmerising
morning,
The birds fluttering above the boats,
The boatmen rushing, untying the ropes,
O what an enigmatic view of chaos and hope!
It is only here that you find solace in
commotion,
The Kashivishwanath temple, the
Dashashwamedh ghat, Assi ghat,
There is no dearth of people amalgamating in
the voices of Arati,
Pouring their devotion, boundless, hearty!
The city is lively, the streets are full,
Yet tranquility thrives, where sages chant
still.
The kids dressed as Shiva and Parvati play,
Their innocence lighting up the winding
pathways.
The evenings are colourful, the lamps set
afloat,
Reflecting on the river,
Banaras, where time moves at its own pace,

Holding onto tradition with a warm
embrace.
A city of wonder, of life, of eternal grace,
By the ghats, the soul finds its rightful space.

How human are we?

We hate each other and party together,
We live with each other and draw the lines,

We divide and we multiply,
On humans, we rely,
We like some of them, we leave some of them,
We hate some of them, we kill some of them!

We cannot live without each other,
We run together, we rob together,
We cry together, we sob together,
We still do not accept many of us,
We label them and disown them,
We throw them, we push them away,
We blindly trust them and we crush them
away!

We do not like some of others existence,
We have shown a lot of resistance,
We love few animals, we dislike some,
We sleep with some, we eat some,
We use some we dispose some,

We sideline few, we impose some,
We rest with few, we are at our best with few,
We cajole some, we distract some,
We boycott some, we attract some!

What is the faith of our race,
With so many contradictions, so many
actions,
Are we going to expand or are we going to
collapse?
It is only dependent on one fact if it can be
quantified,

How human are we?

Strong as thunderstorm

Yes, I might have appeared weak then,
Yes, I was not in the best of my shape then,
My feet swollen,My face was tensed,
But trust me,
I was as strong as the thunderstorm!
I had a lot to mourn then,
I had many questions unanswered,
Dreams were haunting me from the past,
My hands shivered at time,
But
I was determined as the war sword!
At times, I felt like giving up,
Yes, I was confused at times,
Should I or should I not,
I wondered many a times,
But trust me,
The only thing I craved for the entire time,
Was to know the truth and sometimes an urge
to get vanished in the crowd,
But guess what,
That is not something I feel anymore!
Months gone by and years are passing by,
I look back at times, shrug my shoulder,

Gaze ahead and tell myself,
The way I handled everything,
Those scary nights,
With tears in my heart but a smile on my
face,
I have made myself proud!

Transversing the tough

Looking at the purple petals, the lush green beauty,
The flowing Bhagirathi, a gush of cool air!
What can be more peaceful than sitting by the stairs
Thinking about everything that I have accomplished And in the process, whatever chose to perish!
I see the sun setting behind the temple, Hear the hymns from the far away town,
A serene symphony that calms all my frown!
The clouds paint the sky with shades of gold, Memories of the trek,
Stories untold, Mountains standing tall, a sight to behold, Nature's embrace, so gentle and bold,
As night falls, the stars begin to gleam, Lost in this moment, it feels like a dream,
The journey within, a silent, flowing stream.

Winding Roads and Wheels - Journey from Manali to Leh

A pedal more, an inch more,
A test of mental strength and resilience,
Wondering when I chose to embark on this quest,
Rational decision or emotional, but here I am!
Amidst these majestic mountains,
Crossing the treacherous passes, Admiring the simplicity of life,
Learning to persevere through the strife.
Some days were sunlit, some windswept,
Some brought reluctant rains wept.
The roaring waterfalls in Sissu,
the tiny tea stall at Zing Zing Bar,
Boiled potatoes for dinner, Tents pitched in Sarchu,
the straight, unforgiving roads of More plains,

Monasteries standing serene, Lakes
shimmering along the way,
The grueling uphill of Baralacha-la, the fun
ghost stories,
the exhilarating downhill of Lato,
Snow-clad peaks, mesmerizing and grand,
Forging bonds with riding partners, steadfast
and grand.
Finally, our dream destination - Leh, the love
of all adventure enthusiasts!
Every drop of sweat, every pedal stroke -
worth it all.

Why I chose to run Ladakh Half Marathon?

Motherhood brought a bittersweet
transformation,
A new world to navigate while searching for
the old me, In a bid to rediscover my identity
and reclaim my stride,
I set my sights on the Ladakh Half Marathon,
Nine months lay ahead, a fresh journey to
undertake,
The beginning of a new year, the crafting of a
bold challenge, Casting away fear, embracing
the unknown.
I learned to accept my body's evolution,
to stop chasing the past, And to forge a new
version of myself.
Each day, I pushed my limits, ran many local
races,
Faced moments of disheartening doubt,
Wondering if I could ever run like before.
Yet, determination fueled my spirit; progress
came into view,

Strengthened not just in body, but in mind and soul.
I embraced the challenge with an unyielding resolve,
Staying disciplined, making sacrifices, Aware of the price I had to pay.
Through sunlit days and gloomy nights,
I persevered, conquering each mile with unwavering will.
Reaching the vibrant heights of Ladakh,
Breathing in the crisp mountain air,
Surrounded by the breathtaking landscape, I felt alive and free,
The journey was not just physical, But a transformative odyssey of self-discovery.
And when I crossed the finish line, The sense of accomplishment was profound,
Not once, not twice, but I conquered my goal, thrice!

Olive

And with a beaming smile, she opened the
door,
Just above the cafe, where she handles every
chore.
Our meeting felt as though it were just
yesterday,
Despite a full year that had slipped away.
The place carried the same vibe, the same
aroma,
I was welcomed with a warm hug and her
eyes' big sparkle in panorama.
I waited at the cafe, watching kids play in the
masjid's court,
Right in front of the cafe, a lively fort.
The windy weather, a mesmerizing evening,
Bustling streets, hidden cafes, footpaths
teeming,
Fruit sellers by the side, chit-chatting, Trying
to sell their beautifully handwoven bandanas,
Then she arrives with a hot mug of coffee,
Expressions clear—so much to share, a
dialogue ready.

We spoke of her children and so much more,
Stories unfolding from a rich store,
I bid her goodbye, we performed our ritual,
Clicked our selfie, a moment to cherish
eternal,
Hoping to see her again next year,
Friendship that surpasses today and
tomorrow's sphere,
Something to cherish for life, a moment of
love and care,
Her name is Olive, a bond beyond compare.

The uncanny concealer

I wasn't looking good.
You all said I had a plain face.
So, I put on my makeup. Hid the tears behind
the crimson blush.
 Covered the marks of my past with a few
more strokes of kohl,
 Blended the harsh words with a bold
foundation,
 (Thinking, now I'm strong).
A streak of liner traced the wrinkle of worry
carved by haunted dreams.
 I thought I had crafted a face you would
embrace.
But you'd talk about how naturally beautiful I
was before,
 And how awful I looked now—hidden
behind layers of color.
 Where is the true me?
 Who is this person you've helped paint?
It might sound bitter, but here's the truth:
 I wasn't the artist of my own image.
 It was you who drew me.

Reflections at Shanti Stupa

As I sat holding my cup of tea, gazing at the
horizon,
The lavender petals waving as the wind sets in
motion,
Yellow pollen inside, reflecting the color of
the sun,
Guest houses looked so tiny from above, like
dreams undone.
The air getting colder, cheerful children
nearby, Subliming sunrays,
the day's final goodbye, The place looks the
same, as if I was here yesterday!
Shanti Stupa, a serene embrace for tourists in
Leh's sway.
White as clouds, blue and purple designs at
its base,
The mighty Buddha inside, a calm and sacred
space,
A panoramic view that leaves one in a daze!

The garland of mountains, the green patch of
Ganglas.
Winding trails nearby, weaving stories
untold,
Into thin air, yet feels so full, bold and old,
As night falls, the Stupa stands, tranquil and
grand,
Holding moments of peace in its silent hand.

By the Ghats of Banaras

The magenta hues of the mesmerising
morning,
The birds fluttering above the boats,
The boatmen rushing, untying the ropes,
O what an enigmatic view of chaos and hope!
It is only here that you find solace in
commotion,
The Kashivishwanath temple, the
Dashashwamedh ghat, Assi ghat,
There is no dearth of people amalgamating in
the voices of Arati,
Pouring their devotion, boundless, hearty!
The city is lively, the streets are full,
Yet tranquility thrives, where sages chant
still.
The kids dressed as Shiva and Parvati play,
Their innocence lighting up the winding
pathways.
The evenings are colourful, the lamps set
afloat,
Reflecting on the river,
Banaras, where time moves at its own pace,

Holding onto tradition with a warm
embrace.
A city of wonder, of life, of eternal grace,
By the ghats, the soul finds its rightful space.

Aachi

As far as you see, you see brown mountains,
and snow on top of each of them, yet no
shade, the sun - big and bright, walking
alongside,
We were on our bike, witnessing the early
morning chills,
Hands frozen, eyes hopeful, embracing the
cutting wind.
After halting for a few minutes at the
Khardungla pass,
Snapped a few pictures, we continued to
ride.
The twists and turns of the mighty
mountains,
The steep uphills and the treacherous
downhills,
Reading the BRO boards, admiring the
beauty,
Thanking people on our way, the army guards
posted on duty.
Somewhere in the midst of Khardung village,
We were in search of Aachi!

My friend was looking for her to express gratitude,
For offering him to stay while he was preparing for an ultra marathon,
A place serene and calm, just glory of simplicity and higher altitude!
We stopped by a couple of places, Asking about her, 72 kilometers of ride,
only to see her and wish her. And after a few moments of search,
there she was, Giggling and chatting with her friends near a tree.
Hugged us and invited us to join her gang.
They were busy, Braiding stories of seasons, singing songs of the hills.
Her laughter rippled, soft yet strong, It felt like home, though we'd been gone so long.
She served us tea, earthy and sweet,
Tashi our canine friend was also enjoying the treat,
Stories poured out, tales of courage and defeat.
Gratitude brimmed in her eyes, unspoken yet loud,
In her humble abode, we felt so proud.

We bid her goodbye, her blessings our guide,
A journey enriched by the warmth she
supplied.
Aachi, so pure and so kind, Her spirit, her
smile—we'll forever rewind.

Echoes of horizon!

You are not dreaming, not sleeping, to get up
and achieve your dream,
Or are you sleeping and dreaming, so that you
can dream your dream?
When the rains are heavy but the veins are
dry,
When the wind is blowing and nobody is
around,
Never give up but try!
Thoughts as high as a mountain, values as
deep as an ocean,
Energy as positive as sunrise and a heart full
of emotions!
A moment of peace and a life full of hues,
Focus on your dream as life gives no cues,
Keep striving for what you what to achieve,
and don't get bogged down while many will
be pulling you down,
Even an extra step will contribute, do not
worry, do not cry over,
Never give up, try but try!!

Unseen Scars, Unspoken Weights

Lifting those backpacks—fifteen kilograms of relentless weight,
Hiking through rhododendrons, lost in the beauty of the trail,
Do we ever pause to weigh the burden of others' judgments we carry?
We wince at blisters that mar our feet after endless miles,
Yet overlook the deeper scars left by those who try to pull us down.
We collapse at the dawn, tracing the imprints of others' journeys,
Waiting impatiently for the day to dissolve into night.
But do we grow weary of the way we let people trespass our lives,
Shaping our steps, dimming our light, and tethering our freedom?

Flowing through Life

Does life get defined by the challenges in front of you?
 Or by the heap of problems you've already cut through?
 Is it the dreams you chase tomorrow?
 Or the faded memories you carry from past sorrows?
Is life defined by the broken pieces you've managed to put together?
 Or by the people you believe you'll hold close forever?
 Do you stop to appreciate the first light of the day?
 Do you marvel at the hum of the bee or the waves of the ocean?
 Do you gaze at the sand, shining bright under the sun?
Does it need to be grand to be beautiful?
 Or can it simply be beautiful by being exactly what it is?
Let life define its own beauty—without boundaries, without limits.

Let it flow and take its own shape, unfettered and free.
Stay positive. Meditate. Enjoy the journey.

www.ingramcontent.com/pod-product-compliance
Lightning Source LLC
LaVergne TN
LVHW021306200726